QUANTUM ENTANGLEMENT

APALACHEE PRESS

QUANTUM ENTANGLEMENT

POEMS

Carol Lynne Knight

APALACHEE PRESS

Tallahassee, Florida

2010

Cover art: *Bright Window,* digital painting by Carol Lynne Knight
Author photograph: Albert J. Hall
Cover and text design: Carol Lynne Knight (knight02@comcast.net)
Type Styles: titles and text set text in Adobe Garamond Pro;
      ornament from Bickham Script Pro

Library of Congress Cataloging-in-Publication Data
Quantum Entanglement by Carol Lynne Knight – First Edition
ISBN – 978-0-940821-09-5
Library of Congress Cataloging Card Number – 2010927740

This publication is sponsored in part
by a grant from the Council on Culture & Arts
for Tallahassee/Leon County.

Apalachee Press Inc. is a nonprofit corporation.
For personal orders and information write to:
Apalachee Press
P.O. Box 10469
Tallahassee, Florida 32302
Web site: www.apalacheereview.org
E-mail: new.apalachee.press@gmail.com
Published in the United States
by Apalachee Press
Tallahassee, Florida
First Edition, 2010

For Rob,
most profound evidence of my existence

Contents

Acknowledgments

Grateful acknowledgment to the publications in which these poems first appeared, sometimes in different form:

Apalachee Review: "A Penny for Your Thoughts"
Comstock Review: "Fog"
Epicenter: "Binary"
HazMat: "My Brothers,"
Iconoclast: "Party Girl"
Lousiana Literature: "After Angels in America, Part 1"
Northwest Florida Review: "Sonata" (as "Banquet")
Parthenon West: "A Bell, My Breast, My Flesh,"
www.poetsagainstthewar: "Now and Then"
Redactions: "Without Words"
Tampa Review: "Pollination"
Tar River Review: "Sandwich"

"Lift" appeared in the anthology *The Poets Guide to the Birds,* edited by Judith Kitchen and Ted Kooser (Anhinga Press).

"Naming" appeared in the anthology *Beloved on the Earth,* edited by Jim Perlman, Deborah Cooper, Mara Hart, and Pamela Mittlefehldt (Holy Cow! Press).

"Electric Hair" appeared in the anthology *North of Wakulla,* edited by Mary Jane Ryals and Donna Decker (Anhinga Press).

No book is written alone. Every page is entangled with out past history, friends, influences, kindnesses, and misfortunes. I wish to thank those who have helped me along the way.

I first want to thank Mary Jane Ryals and Michael Trammell for accepting and nurturing this book. They are true adventurers in the world, literary and otherwise.

Mary Jane and Donna Decker chose the poem that ends this book for an anthology many years ago — my first introduction to the lively writing community in Tallahassee.

My ambassador into many things literary is Rick Campbell and Anhinga Press. I thank him for his friendship, generosity, and visionary mind. Through the press, I have had the good fortune to work with many wonderful writers over the years — an experience that has enriched my literary life.

A remarkable group of writers in Tallahassee has been the core support of my writing life. I am grateful to Donna Decker, Melanie Rawls, Laura Newton, and Mary Jane Ryals, who read the first drafts of these poems and several versions of the manuscript, all with care and insight.

My thanks to the Hambidge Center for the Arts for affording me time to shape and edit this book, and also to paint the image on the front cover.

I wish to thank Diane Wakoski and Naomi Shihab Nye, whose kind words grace the cover, for their careful read and wise suggestions. Many years ago, Diane's *Medea the Sorceress* sent me in a new direction, searching the cosmos for many of the words that appear here.

No one arrives without parents. I am grateful to mine — Gene and Sonia Visser — for nurturing my artistic life and their patience with my questioning and rebellions. I keep returning to their story for grounding.

Some Notes on Quantum Entanglement

When two quantum-scale objects, like atoms or nuclei, are entangled, performing an action on one instantaneously affects the other even if vast distances separate the entangled objects.

> "The Question of Quantum Chaos: What We Know,"
> Veronique Greenwood, seedmagazine.com, Dec. 14, 2009

Inherent to quantum mechanics are seeming paradoxes that blur the distinctions between particles and waves, portray all events as matters of probability rather than deterministic destiny and place a particle in a state of ambiguity that makes it potentially two or more things, or in two or more places, at once.

> "Quantum on Quantum: Entangled photons validate Feynman's vision
> for simulating nature," Charles Petit, *Science News.* Feb. 27, 2010

A quantum superposition is a state in which a particle, such as a photon or atom, exists simultaneously in two locations. Entanglement, which Albert Einstein called "spooky action at a distance," allows particles to share information even if they are physically separated.

> "Caltech Physicists Propose Quantum Entanglement for Motion
> of Microscopic Objects," www.media.caltech.edu, Dec. 21, 2009

QUANTUM ENTANGLEMENT

I

ETHER

After "Angels In America, Part I"

Angels in America

often leap from cliffs because we are so boring —
they are appalled by what we watch on television

and in the end, would prefer the drama of sunsets
to the confessions of talk show hosts.

are sometimes lost, and sleep on the drive-in roof
at Sonic, craving strawberry milkshakes.

gather our missing socks from dryers and clotheslines,
give them to nesting birds and homeless shelters.

stay in the attics of single women
with two cats — they know they will be fed.

Angels in America

frequently join parades, kiss Mardi Gras beads
and candy as it flies into the crowd,

rest their infinite hands on the empty shoulders
of fathers whose children no longer ride there.

build towers on obscure hillsides, welding souls
to the steel, riveting the past to doorways.

Angels in America

embellish their reports, assign meaning
and beauty to cruel and senseless acts.

wander through Wal-Mart, taking inventory of souls
coming through the door who have no where else to go,

following mothers with long lists: socks, diapers, hairspray,
training bras and Bic pens — what everyone thinks they need.

Angels in America

count our desires, acts of redemption, our heresies,
lies, assumptions, our ethical dilemmas and suicides.

tally what should be taken away,
to balance our prayers with what is offered.

String Theory

In nature, there is a single variety of string-like object. The string is not "made up of anything," rather, it is basic and other things are made up of it.
> — Sunil Mukhi,
> *String Theory and the Unification of Forces*

How my skin sags and billows!
  But one square inch is wondrous
    down to the charity of bones.
The weight of daily consequence lifts.
The knot of sorrow holds the perfect stone
   in suspension, glowing testament of angels
    who sometimes whisper into the extreme isolation
     of urban transport — their voices
      in the whine of brakes,
      the empty bus —
the acrobat of desire somersaulting under lamp posts,
lights singing an aria on empty streets,

Fish and stone, frog and snake — flesh exposed,
  complicated in the rhythm of rope.
Intention dangling from a phone cord on the nightstand,
a series of small scratches that itch
  with the healing, but never bleed.
Sanctuary of water, dulcet splash
   of the oar dipping into reverence.
Knowing the struggle
  of being tethered by one foot
   binds us into a circle.

Anti-Matter

The collision of anti-matter and matter destroys the matter.

i.
I confess,
I don't quite believe in the Periodic Table,
that we can count protons —
and now scientists have discovered anti-matter,
anti-hydrogen with positrons whirling
their little plus signs around anti-protons.
And the comings and goings of the substance
of our lives — things we thought so simple —
depend on to be solid, could be
the opposite.

I confess, I close the closet door
before I lie down, even with the lights on,
shut out the monsters wearing my clothes,
shutter the confusion of shoes hiking
through a chaos hidden inside.

ii.
Confess,
and break my heart — tell me the details,
so I can picture your betrayal completely,
can be overcome by it, obsessed by it.
If I admit my guilt, after absorbing yours,
what particle of my hair, my skin, my soul,
will you carry away with your absolution?

iii.
I listen,
and your ragged voice confesses —
places a brown feather of guilt between my fingers.
It doesn't seem so heavy.

But after all your confessions spill into this empty room,
shift their dark weight into my hands,
I can no longer listen, offer absolution,
or forgive my own silence.

Lost Poem

I lost the poem for today
and I apologize — losing poetry is like losing civilization.
But of course, the poem wasn't quite a poem yet,
just a story with poetic possibilities
about my mother and her drugged visions at the hospital,
but that bitch muse has been taunting me
with half lines and semi-ideas for months.
Sometimes, I beat her to the ground,
pull a poem from her belly like a psychotic surgeon.
Caesarian poems are never quite what I had in mind —
sometimes good, but unnaturally shaped,
bleeding from the rusty knife that excised the words,
never breathing in the proper measured rhythm.

Hah! I hate poems about writing poems!
The process should be secret and magical,
like the muse has pitched the words from heaven
and the sequence has fallen on my head.
Maybe she is distracted by politics
and the never ending stupidity she sees.
It must take infinite energy to resist battering
politicians who create visions so horrific
that even the most callous can only weep.

I never realized the muse
is not exclusively mine.
Maybe she has been away —
holding the head of an Iraqi poet in her lap,
stroking a bruised cheek, whispering,
Write, write.

Birds, Austin

1
These birds are rude,
squawking, whistling, creening,
like the cousin who drinks too much
and heaves his voice into the wedding toast —
                    crass tenor of his laugh.

At first we think the birdcalls are recorded
to give the stolid convention center some ambience.
Then the light shifts —
sun slips behind the downtown skyline
and avian shadows appear in trees,
hundreds of birds hooting exotic, metallic cries —
no angelic chorus, but raucous party birds
ready for the city at night, its house of blue neon.

Three kinds of grackles, says the woman at the next table,
picking at her salad and flirting with my son,
            who studiously reads a local tabloid.
                    She keeps talking — he turns another page …
            Why isn't a local guy with that longish blond hair I like
                    telling me about bird species,
                            telling me his afternoon is free?

2
We could destroy the silence in this hotel room,
            in this duveted, sleep numbered, wi-fied haven
                    we don't even have to clean,
this room where embarrassment
                    is swept up every morning.
We could paint our footprints on the ceiling.

3
With my heart of broken trees, my palm of bent twigs,
I could fly, but it would be stop-motion fake.

See, there are strings attached.
The puppeteer keeps scissors in his left hand.

Petals fall like broken wings while I sleep.
I tell my dream hand to open the taxi door.

We are city dwellers,
          skin stained by neon in this dream.
We juggle cigarettes and sable paint brushes.
I can play the piano, my hands find melody
              without lessons, without practice.

When I was young, and rode through these streets,
I thought I would live on the fifth floor.
There would be a staircase, an arched window
        spilling light across the landing,
              orchids on the roof, a coffee cup posed
                    and waiting in the café at the corner,
paint freckling my hair,
an ultramarine smear riding my left cheek,
my fingers lifting like butterflies into the skyline,
hanging from a handle bar moon.

          4
It's a story that could happen,
        but I don't float now, don't fly.
I walk carefully around corners,
        and there is no time to pose with an espresso,
        no deep pocket minutes to fling into the street,
        no stories of the angel that died still surprised by evil,
              the permanence of deeds,
              by the transcendence of the hand
                    still reaching down to pull us up.

Liar II

I told you once that I was a liar
    and you believed me.
That your face is clouds. That clouds become your face.
That mist rising from fields on a cool September morning
    reminds me of your face.

Your face — when I can't remember its contours,
    when its curves have softened into clouds,
and you are disappearing, the day becomes electric,
    a searing wound of minutes.

That this peach is suddenly a carnal object,
    desired and consumed.
    That this peach may or may not become a cloud
but in its consummation,
    sadly must be eaten.
The full moon, blushing like a peach,
    just before dark floats over the parking lot,
    tames no one with its full face,
        toys with the secrets we carry —
            burdens swarthy, sweet, and delicate
        as clouds that become your face.

On days without clouds, without suggestion
    that you might still exist, lies creep from beneath the sheets,
    burden the blankets with confession, with false logic.

Bathe in this mist, this future cloud. Walk into
    its temporary cloak, its ambience damned and threadbare.

I lied about this cloud, my heart — it is broken,
    it is mended, it is a spider.
Declension defines me.
    I lied, am lying, will lie.
        Believe me.

Variations On Dimension

*Although they have not identified them, physicists have
predicted that, mathematically, there must be ten dimensions.*

The finger-widths of air hidden in crinolines,
layers of stiff lace shaping the space
around my body, trapping illusions that surround me.

The spread of my hips at thirteen,
bone jutting farther into the world,
snagging door jams before I know my place.

The height of my son penciled on the wall,
scratches of memory I paint around for years,
framing his childhood on a vertical surface.

The depth of grief, weeping on a cellular level —
mapping the distance through protoplasm to my heart,
the ache of blood scraping the walls of my veins.

Time draped like power lines across my path,
a photon necklace that monkeys skywalk,
that adorns and gradually chokes me.

Springtime bursting fuchsia, kaleidoscope
of burgeoning desire. Egg breaking open,
exposing the double helix of inheritance.

Path of angels, weaving between my feet
like hungry cats, tripping me with distraction,
with the white fur of their silence.

Behind the mirror, a woman brushes a left-sided part
into my hair. When I leave, her smudged image drifts
into an identical room, leads her own life until I return.

To become what has no dimension — my father
in heaven pruning his roses, lies down
without pain — asleep with the gods.

The boundaries of infinity, horizon at the rim of everything.
We could fall off, be consumed by dragons that defy dimension,
divine beyond our comprehension, our words.

Paradox

Curled viper of paradox sleeps in my hands.
Moon hisses, slides into the trees.
Let it fall, how would you stop it?

Seeking the one safe place,
that bed of curling arms and legs,
a blanket for regret.

Mortality like a shovel balanced
over an open pit, heavy with dirt.
Let it fall, how can you stop it?

Trumpet in the darkness soaring,
blister of sound in the frying-pan night,
sequined tux, fingers singeing heaven,

glamour with a whiff of cigarette,
triumph of mind over smoke — breathe,
and let it go. How could you keep it?

Bread that leavens to be eaten,
how can you stop the urge to rise,
the paradox of collapse?

Let it rise.
How can you stop
the moon, the bread, the fist?

WITHOUT WORDS

When we were not speaking,
I wondered how to tell you without words
where I was going, how I would walk
outside and breathe slowly to catch my heart
before it raced into the swamp of singing
that prowls about us.

It was before we invented fire,
before words, before the shape of words.

When we did not speak,
the air still burst with visions,
animals purring, yowling,
chaos parting air and water,
the moon rising from underground gardens.
When we did not speak,
our fists formed meaning —
unmistakable, furious
curled into our mouths,
      too blue to utter,
      too red to grasp,
      too green to listen.
We wove baskets of grief,
killed ferrets and doves,
skinned them and ate.

When we learned to speak,
the words became round beads
we put on strings, chains of meaning
to hang around our necks —
too many syllables rivering
through our veins like prophecy.
We invented god to interpret the heavens for us,
realized our tongues are *small* instruments
if we wish to speak to the stars.

Thunder

We change roles as we roll over one another
        male, female reigning in a rain storm —
            you the thunder, I the lightning,
light and call, brash cymbal,
brash desire, wild impatience,
longing, long awaiting
            the deceit of your tongue.

You think you are alone in your thoughts
but I am your secret, a fold of flesh,
the unfolding of your truest companion.
You will return when you find
        you have lost the palm of your hand,
            the other half of gesture,
                the encryption of your desire.

We reach into the stutter, savor the echo
                falling from our tongues,
you and I, clatter of words,
stones on glass, thunder
            coming, fractured —
the other side of your hand,
                a clap away.

*… the quantum connection between two particles can persist even
if they are on opposite sides of the universe. From the standpoint of
their entanglement, notwithstanding the many trillions of miles of
space between them, it's as if they are right on top of each other.*
— Brian Greene,
*The Fabric of the Cosmos: Space, Time,
and the Texture of Reality*

If you measure love's path,
pairs of electrons that spin ambiguously
suddenly become a marriage.

If I count the freckles on your back while you sleep, shine
a flashlight under the sheets, you wake and turn counter
clockwise — toward me, if I sleep on the left side

and dream that our love is quantified
with decimal points, even as it flees,
and touch mutates into observation.

If I tell you the world is flying apart, it could be true,
theoretically. But this morning the backyard green
rises, surrounds me with tendrils of prayer,

and the first woodpecker of spring drills
into the pecan tree outside the window.
Feathers on his red cap — so smooth.

This week we dwell in pollen —
amber rivers coursing in the driveway
after rain, sallow clouds sifting through trees.

We all weep without sadness.
An exaggeration of air hovers,
blanketing pickup trucks and limousines.

We have all been chosen for pollination.
In June, we will birth azaleas,
and dogwood puppies will fill our arms.

See how the world is painted yellow with desire.

Exit

Forever has an escape clause,
      you said, with eyes closed,
      sitting at the end of my bed,
          pulling on a woolen sock.
I know, because my eyes flashed open,
lashes flying across your bare shoulder.

I know this, in the way that cats sometimes
fly out the door and sometimes return,
      or allow themselves to be plucked up
      as they chew the grass they sought,
but they can disappear forever —
      leaving only a matte of gray fur
          where they slept.
I know this in an elemental way —
      if there is no way out, there is no way in.

Why mention the escape clause now?
What just happened to our bodies should overshadow
      love's legalities,
         although the brush of leaving
         had painted a small corner in my mind,
         coloring the spaces you occupy
         with vague mental furniture.
There are ways to fill the gaps,
      redecorate the heart's desire —
         mahogany door stops, silken Chinese screens.

If you open a door, you can shut it,
      back away from the entrance,
         entranced by the detritus of passion
           or anxious to run —
if I can love you forever,
and the equal, but opposite action follows,
      am I describing *never,*

or a winged creature careening
through love's dark hall?

Is love an intransitive verb,
silhouette without nuance,
a single hair left on an unwashed shirt,
neurons curled up like kittens
lost in a forest of obligation?

We are Escher diagrams — interlocking hands
seemingly separate, but undeniably entwined.
There is no intimacy
if together, we climb into a prison,
its iodine fear of being cut,
flow of clarion blood.

The coming in, the going out —
embrace of possibility, coitus of escape.
If you leave — I move the bed,
risk the unfamiliar alignment
of sleeping by the window,
discover the light breaking dawn,
jump through the glass,
and arrive at a point of departure,
conjure up the perfect moment to say goodbye.

Palms wave like hands of the sun,
rustle their fronds as wind moves into a perfect place,
a tropical kind of dénouement.

A home has doors.
I leave and return.
My heart has a ladder.

One hundred years ago,
      only a cheetah could go this fast.
Now I hurl down a road
      on fire with refraction,
      with the idleness of sorrow,
      morning angst still hovering in the ditch,
         billboards flashing like high-speed lures,
            exits and destinations
         almost extraterrestrial.

I carry a burden of genetic appropriation,
      rolling marathon of loud music, six-lane cloister of sound.
Smoke of memory unfurls
      in a swale of ragged black ribbons,
         a breaking heart braking hard.

How fast can you go, how long will the road
      unroll its redemption?
At the last Dairy Queen, a chance atonement —
      vanilla obligation drips on to the floor mat,
         engages the gearshift,
         throws the approaching squall into reverse.

A wheel of adversity, of blind driving semi,
      horn of triumph, axles of automatic redaction
         dissect your compulsion for speed
            with gravity and flame,
transforms you into wind,
      thrusts you like a meteor
         past forgiveness.

Stopped at the red light on White Drive,
I am pulling words from the wires
above the intersection.

Sparrows fold themselves along the line,
brief commas, barely punctuating
the morning commute below.

They stutter along the wire
by twos and threes, uneven beat
in a rushed morning song.

Spreading wings, lifting
into the late gray dawn as it drifts
above the signal. Unfolded,

they become a dark fluency,
a flock of words, a coda written
low across the ashen clouds,

We are the prayer in your mouth.

Secret Body

This is my secret body,
draped in Atlantic seaweed,
stung by tentacles of jellyfish, by deer flies and fire ants,
truss of my soul, keeper of my first kiss,
upended in a junior high backseat tryst,
sarcophagus of school girl terrors, reliquary of disease,
stroked by lovers I don't remember,
chased by memories that overtake me at intersections,
   their blond hands, solid pricks, veins like straw.

These days, I reveal my body to strangers — scheduled,
   clinical one night stands.
Here is my breast, my vagina,
   an exemplary artery, a vein waiting to be opened —
all yours for the hour, all yours with payment due.

Imagine my skin like glass, window into the muscle of heart,
intricacy of arteries consuming pulse,
concert of lungs rising and falling,
my puzzling corporeal presence:
   tectonic shifts of cellular belief,
   identity crisis at the atomic level,
   maze-like paths in my cerebral vault

where whispered tales slur into drunken headlights
    and blurred vision.
Old secrets in tight dresses
now appear down the hall, wrapped in flannel robes.

In heaven, I hear, there are no bodies,
no secrets, no skin, no cleavage.
No sex. Maybe I am there.

I am telling my secrets.
   It is like a touch.

For rp

A search for double spaces,
closing them like a fist this morning,
        and all the double hyphens
that must be joined, made whole —
the sigh of em dashes,
a space on either side for breath.
        The mourning is in the design.

Though finishing is the goal,
I am not ready to commit this file
        to god's hands.
There could be missing page numbers,
an errant space before a comma,
all those things that should not appear
        on a beloved page
                if you have paid careful attention.
Punctuation like a caul,
        a dream of perfection that persists,
so much grammar
lost to the open white sky of this winter —

a page that keeps turning to be proofed,
the least word noted,
a period nudged into its final place,
all the margins examined, no syllable
        stretching beyond its boundaries —
although to bind this text so tightly
        seems an ironic obligation.

The opaque white of the page shifts
like clouds. If you search for proof,
it is not in the sky, but seems
        it should be written
                just above the horizon.

II

RHETORICAL QUESTIONS

Good Morning/How Are You?

While applying my mascara, I had an existential crisis.
I imagined my life without coming here today, or any day.
I crept in the back door, hoping you wouldn't ask.

The radio announced the hunger season,
the body counts, the IEDs —
I switched on Leonard Cohen to cheer me up.
I am wearing clothes fashioned by a boa constrictor.
        My hair has become a physics theory.

I was too distracted to drive —
        lucky for you the car I just parked
                next to yours
                    knows how to get here on its own.
My mind is still in pajamas,
falling off the last cliff of consciousness.

I am sleepwalking into the sixth dimension.
        Its confusion of gravity has me baffled
            and excited. I assumed the earth
would always confine me.

It's complicated — veins are involved, and feet,
        a subatomic rattle in the dash board.
I am wondering if quantum entanglement allows me
        to be here, and still go home.

This is a hard question — can I get back to you?

How Was Your Day?

Dawn trailing light like a forgetful angel,
carelessly dropping feathers in the driveway.
First syllables — aphasic utterings,
somewhat feline. Shelter of sheets lifting.
I rise at this ambiguous hour —

first steps, a stuttering into dust,
belief in the coming day ethereal,
the sun a wild prediction,
like a dog straining at the leash,
not quite tame.

There was a darkness in the afternoon.
Did I dream a storm, lamps flickering,
unlit avenues detouring through the house,
lightning billowing at the windows,
thunder startling the glass?

Dinner thaws under the faucet,
cold and waiting, still blue fingered,
song of water cascading in the sink.
Evening meal, a shared providence,
communion that binds us.

Twilight of sleep, TV angel falling through
a cathedral ceiling, his body splaying swan like.
How I recall the splendor of his wings,
the artifice of feathers arcing across the aisle —
and not the play of death.

Where Are You Going?

This slow day
driven by a separate heart
        needs quickening,
needs the bright glint of sun
skating on your watch.
This landscape needs
        the rough hills of your hand
riding the steering wheel —
our atoms on the same trajectory,
painted with red clover, wild
        on moving glass,
your shadow clichéd,
a French metaphor for following.
Lavender petals
        drift easily on the wind —
                willows and pipers.
How the revolution turns
highway into choir,
a benediction of reason,
race of heart.

I'm going with *you*.

What's The Difference?

Between a door fallen shut at two in the morning
and a key deftly turned in a lock of hair.

If you care, or don't — I'm still inhaling rain,
still hooked on your blue green fish-flopping love.

Between a promise and prayer — the atom parsed
to its basic despair or pleas in the hunger season.

Between withholding a word that will heal
and a deliberate slap, delivered without spite.

If I love a sinner or hate their sin, when
they perceive my embrace as expiation.

What's the difference between paranoid and pursued,
entangled in comic intrigues of the heart.

Between the curl of the king's smug smile
and the sadness of his queen.

In the bride I was and the bride I am not, princess
or clown, never adorned in white ruff or lace.

A fiery kiss, and flame I recall.

Don't I Know You?

I was a billboard along I-75
for Café Risque — eventually fading,
my face fell into the trees.

I was a movie once,
directors reeling through my soul,
all my clichés unraveling.

My name is buried in a dozen books,
pages of demons and dialogue
before you find me.

I have been digitally disassembled.
You may have been spammed
with my binary code.

I was a poster child
for early detection.
Maybe you are my doctor.

On the radio, I made sounds
like a cat you once knew,
my voice a dusky scar.

TV cameras found my face
at the courthouse —
co-star of a slow news day.

I have been folded into the newspaper,
misquoted and misspelled —
perhaps you recognize the typos.

There I am,
across the room:
        the one you know.

Can I Buy You A Drink?

I have an obvious thirst, evidence
of a dry heart, a desert of desire.

Fill me up — I am an empty bottle, doubt
like tequila's worm, curling at the bottom.

Pour me out — it's like buying a kiss
at the circus, all fanfare and trapeze.

My glass is sweating, cool but nervous,
sliding along the bar — a lot like you.

I *could* swallow it, my throat wants work, wants
to choke the indiscretions that keep slipping out.

Will there be dancing? Clinch and sway?
Or more like kickboxing to music?

What kind of commitment will I be drinking?
Does it expire at midnight, or linger till sunrise?

Is this a loaves-and-fishes transaction?
Will the morning-after be my salvation?

I could say yes to you; in these rum & coke shadows,
this neon haze, you're almost handsome.

Can You Hear Me?

I drowse when the moon is inking the trees
and streetlights draw shadows on the driveway.
Do you hear me dream your name,
the sigh that is your appellation?

Can you hear the slow division of cells,
my skin sloughing off, the knitting
of molecules, the peculiar parsing
of atoms — my origins, so infinite?

With your closed eyes,
do you hear me bow,
pushing air toward the floor
as my torso bends to honor?

Do you hear my lamp exhale its light at eleven,
the stirring of sheets as I prepare for sleep?
Can you hear each prayer float
into the moon's small eye,

hear the gods intrude? Celestial speech:
small vibrations that barely move
a dragon's wing, sonic booms —
catastrophes of desire.

Can you hear me bargain with time, with gravity,
bending night to ineluctable day. For now
my name is *fire* — can you hear the flames
wick wind from the cave of your heart?

Can you hear me in the tyranny
of this syllable: *no,*
this phrase: *not now,*
this poem: *never?*

A Penny For Your Thoughts?

I was about to close my eyes and imagine
a body still young, but not so stupid —
a little fish that knew it was a fish.

I have been letting go of rational thought lately,
and basically, I have not been thinking
in the sense, or non-sense you are asking about.

I was thinking about the lack of transcendence
in this house and wondering if a new tablecloth
would put me in touch with the universe.

I was hoping I could force the latest hurricane
into the mid Atlantic, twist its course
like a lock of hair winding on my finger.

How I cannot overcome gravity without invention,
but could drop a penny into the river
and pretend that it's raining money.

I was wondering if you can embrace someone forever,
or if, after touching, the rage to separate
generates chaos, like a siren in rush hour traffic.

I was picturing a bright swarm
of fireflies glittering my hair —
the collective unconscious in flames.

I was wondering why I spend so much time
drawing a line around myself, marking the difference
between my foot and the floor beneath it,

hoping the line would protect me
from the rumored oneness of thought and anemone,
of eggs that drop from their nest and my odd dreams.

How drawing my hand is easier if I forget
the fingers and draw the air between them.
How I am not air, but its chamber.

If my memory disappears like dream teeth —
floating away on the breath of sleep,
how will I find the empty mouth of morning?

Did You Lose Something?

I lost Ecuador, a word that fell into the sea
and resurfaced on my screen this morning,
returned to my consciousness — iridescent lizard from Galapagos.

I lost minutes, slipping off the table like a silk cloth,
a sheen, a lilting greenish silence.

I lost my virginity on the kitchen floor,
dried macaroni curling under the stove,
a dusty, laid-flat perspective of desire.

I lost two years of marriage.
I always said thirteen,
but in a traffic-light musing
today, I counted on my fingers
and found the missing years, as my thumb
and index finger uncurled from my fist.

Did I lose two years
of the silent treatment, his jaw an angry clench,
or was it dreamy midnight discussions
of a future that never played out?

Lost and taken become odd companions:
what is gone may not be obvious,
        (a memory of birds extinct, flash of recognition,
        then off to the tree tops singing without words)
may not be rare (a car picked clean, no wheels,
        or seats, sad metal carcass in the back lot,
        rusted chariot flattened by thieves).

Whatever has been uttered, fractures —
whole words have gone missing.
Ecuador — a hollow between heart and beat,
ruined symmetry of possession.

I lost my sense of direction, the road curled
like paper burning at the edges, destinations
hidden in the ocean's folded border.

The North Star is torn in half,
like the dark muscle of my heart,
cleft by lies and neglect.

My cat lies near the road in a swale
of unmowed grass, limbs akimbo,
limp with imperfection and impact.

Spiders creep across my forehead,
a web of circumstance tangled
in my hair. I might be poison.

Your words are sand —
how long will they lie on my cheek,
a definition of thirst?

I am no longer famous, my diary
scribbled with ellipses and dashes,
some pages wounded
                with a single ✗.

WHAT ARE YOU THINKING?

I am thinking I should become
a museum and charge admission.

I am thinking that the world will flood
if we turn on all the faucets.

I am dividing my body into profit centers.
I am a cliff pouring birds into the ocean.

I am wondering how long it takes
starfish to regenerate a lost limb.

I am counting the freckles on my left hand,
and hoping my fake fingernails don't fall off.

I am thinking that this kiss
seems parallel to my last kiss,

that I have shaped this embrace
into a familiar desire.

I have forgotten the question.

Bad Boys

Where are Buddy and Buzz and Fred?
Those bad boys I kissed in the back seat,
the boys with cigarettes and duck tails,
motorcycles and James Dean eyes —
always a sucker
for their long hair curling over their collars
their throaty mufflers,
peeling rubber, and popped clutches.

Those bad boys drifting
and taking me with them —
to the drag strip,
to the drive-in,
necking in cemeteries,
necking at the racetrack,
lipstick lost in the rear view mirror,
hands sliding up my thigh,
gear shift jabbing my ribs.
Palm fronds brushing the windshield,
whispering about a one-armed man
who once left his hook dangling
from a car door in this parking lot,
at midnight.

Where Have You Been?

A syllable stopped me at the corner,
handcuffed me to the walk-wait signal.

Smoke lassoed me — breathing its hot conclusion,
I coughed up words from Berlin, choked on the fire.

In a winding hallway, throwing all the switches,
constructing a path of sacred light.

Calling for thunder, and new rain to fall,
drumming my fingers on a tin roof,

In the labyrinth of sorrow — my tears
buoyed me up and I escaped over their waterfall.

In the kitchen. I thought I was a wife. Dishes piled
in the sink — I broke my vow to wash them all.

I stopped by the bank to see my money,
a small stack in the vault of good intention.

Bathing in the luxury of summer ice,
axe of the sun leaning on the back porch.

How strange to be tethered to a singular desire —
I have been to the end of my rope.

Tell Me

Tell me what you don't like about yourself.
— "Nip/Tuck"

That my fingernails are giving up —
splitting before they claw,
that I am cleaved, not cleaving,
placid, not lucid,
that birds sing arias in my backyard
and I cannot parse the lyrics,
that my wings
are still imaginary feathers,
my scars, small
and cryptic ciphers,
that I can't read maps or books
in a car without vertigo,
that I find no rhythm
to trust on the dance floor,
that my hair has gone
on a wild journey without me,
that I don't speak
with a French accent,
but can lie
in any language,
that I haven't had
the best time I ever had (yet),
that I would answer
this question.

Can You Speak a Foreign Language?

Oui, monsieur, I whispered in the backseat
of his hot rod, parked on asphalt or graveyard grass
or even my driveway — my father waiting inside.

Sighed, *Au revoir,* at the end of the night,
my skin awash with the damp scent
of regret and sex and Chanel No. 5.

Queried, *Qué pasa?* as if the answer didn't matter
in the suburbs, ignored the revolution coiling
beneath my bare South Florida feet.

Tossed *C'est la guerre* over my shoulder as I stepped
from a worn out school bus — before Vietnam, before
grenades began exploding during dinnertime newscasts.

Postured, *Qué lastima!* at broken fingernails
and slam book insults, hid my frail daydreams —
caged under short skirts, yet never tamed.

Dreamed, *Carpe diem,* but caved beneath
contingencies, sped through snapshots
now fading in a dingy closeted shoebox.

Loco en la cabeza, we shouted from our car, cruising
the Pizza Palace parking lot — crazy with the blast
of radio rock and a night of flying stars.

C'est la vie, I quipped as melamine food trays
slid down metal rails in my jr. high cafeteria, and I ate
like a wren picking at the mysteries of existence.

Years later, I carried my dark-eyed son into
our corner bodega. *Ayye, qué lindo!* they crooned.
I sighed, *Gracias, gracias* — for beauty's a gift in any language.

III

REFRACTIONS

LIAR

I told you once, I am a liar
and you believed me.
And now, I've become someone else.
The life we dreamed is lost —
        I was the one you trusted
            to change the tragic consequence
                of our breath.

Our love tastes of almonds,
        salty, sweet, somehow bitter,
See, another lie!
        The almonds are not bitter,
            not in the emotional sense I meant.
I am lying, lying, lying.

We are riding in a taxi.
        You kiss me (or kill me).
See, I am lying!
        We were never in a taxi.
        You never kissed me.
        I am still alive,

but I am not dreaming.
I wanted this to happen
        so many times —
            half undressed in the back seat,
            someone we don't know driving.
        We trust him to ignore us,
            to take us where we want to go —
                maybe god is a taxi driver.

As I exit the cab, I let truth slip into the gutter.
I am not waiting anymore. I am lying.

After "Chinese Box"

The box closes, closes again, again.
What lies in this box with the blood jade,
the stone heart, the shadow of the caged bird?
Its secret chambers hide boleros
about the birth of love,
the end of love.

How many times
will the box open,
or silk, veiled in ten-thousand folds,
unfold the map of a face that cannot lie?

If I remember the market
with its butchered meat,
gutted fish pulsing, a young man —
the revolver in his mouth exploding,

I must borrow your illusion —
that dying men are beautiful.
They lie down at the edge of the harbor
listening to the lap of water against the bulkhead,
their skin papering in the sunlight.

They may not wake again,
as porters push their luggage
toward the sea.

At night, fireworks in the harbor
mimic the beauty of war.
Showers of light rain
on the face of god
rippling in the water.
We sip our own illness, derive pleasure
from the wet clear vision of it.
The water bleeds for us.

MY BROTHERS,

when did the summer light falling through
the shawl of poinciana turn blunt, and cold?

Brothers, my sorrow is a claw
when I hear this on the radio,
I want to lay my pencil along the horizon line,
erase all the sunsets after you left — warn you
as you lie on a blanket in a cave of sea grapes,
kissing a girl — warn you
to hold back, to leash the tiger.

Oh, how I turned the page, and you were there,
pasted with black corners into my memory.

The warriors of my generation, bearers of horror
and atrocities, sat beside me in the lunch room,
played co-ed football, broke the rules,
and carried a girl holding the ball
across the goal line, claimed victory,
laughed so hard the game fell apart.

These warriors, my brothers, my lovers
went into the jungle, the sand, the swamp
of war and returned with jaws set, fists tight,
alert, with a belief in necessity,
in imperatives that seem ephemeral now.
With the gauze of paranoia wrapped
around their shoulders,
they thought they wouldn't come home
but tithe their souls in dark terrain.

Momentum,
>child of wings, offspring of angels,
>>misery in updraft,
>>>columns of desire rising through oculus
>>>into cumulus, concubine of restless feathered beasts,
>>>>fallen angels,
>>desperate angels, unable to still their discontent,
>>>urban creatures who flock like gulls to monuments,
>wanting the bronze and stone to remain constant,
>>only to watch it pit with acid rain.
Somnambulant esthetes
>slipper through our dreams,
>>their migrations churning
>>>in a sheath of October leaves.
They follow the monarch butterflies to Kansas, to Mexico —
>perhaps to mate with other winged creatures.
They chew at page corners, eat poems in the rain forest,
>alter consciousness with their slanted charm.
>>Who can say if what they do has happened?

We are their footprints,
>allegory of angelic desires.
They purr, we shout.
>They sing, we wail.
How divine we must be.
>Anomaly of god's children,
>>our entanglements
>>>like tickertape falling from skyscrapers.
Our electric bodies confronting anti-matter —
>everything touched bombarding the next particle,
>>our good intentions
>>>begetting warriors and plagues.
The dominoes of a universe falling over one another
>to find the essence of our sins, our pleasures,

our witness to an unreasonable cosmos.
The gods, too heavy to carry,
            float on barges through our lives.
                We worship the river that carries them,
                    our bellies full of rain and fist.

How many winged creatures will we imagine —
        their feathers bright or sullen, flitting or predatory,
            pushing air into cyclones, grabbing us up
                                as raptured cherubs?

The late sudden stillness of Sunday afternoon,
        angels resting, their murmuring quelled —
        bird calls laze around a far off fence post.
In this pale twilight, they don't insist,
        don't dither over our failures,
            quake and froth at our evil thoughts,
            heave or vomit as we act on them.

Angels gilded, guilt ridden, nap as the sun races toward night
and war hounds slump on the porch a few brief minutes
        before they wake to mortar and shriek.

    We are Phoenix and Bethesda, rising,
        falling, rising,
        prospering in the fire,
        feet touching earth
            in miracles of change.

FIREWORKS

Bodice of the sky
spilling into the bedroom.
Moonlight beads on leaves,

weeps in the city
of my dreams — part New York dark,
part torch lit terrace,

Miami. All stairs
lead to a roof top garden.
Rosary of stars

worries my fingers.
Possession, like a small hand
loosens my shoelace.

Barefoot evensong.
Angels dance in blue corners,
choreography

for feet that would fly.
Ends with a kiss that singes,
midnight and ashes.

LIFT

Minutes ago, a pine branch,
>   singular in its thud, hit the roof.
My cat purred, clicked his tongue.
A cardinal sent his one repeated note
>   skidding over the sprawling lawn.

My broken foot burned and flurried
>   across the pillows.

But now, the backyard is besieged
>   by dozens of dark birds.
They zing from oak to pecan branch,
>   from camellia to fig to pine, whipping
a frenzy into the leaves tethered lightly
>   above the yard in late fall.
Their calls wind chime
>   through startled branches.
They dodge, dip — sweeping the air,
>   possessing the trees.

Dark flitting shadows
>   backlit by the afternoon sun,
>   a frantic gathering.
Look how they dart
>   without colliding,
>   without a leader,
collectively lift into the air —
>   their calls, a flock of sound,
how they multiply
>   in a universe of sequential movement.

Look, I am walking,
>   but it is only enchantment.

Eggs

Today the groceries shifted in the trunk
and the eggs — delicate, candled, blessed —
                did not crack.
I opened the styrofoam carton to find
        all twelve, by luck, still whole.

They could have spilled
        their amber yolks into the bag,
                soaking through, almost cooking
in the mid July oven of the car.

But no, they are still
        nesting undisturbed,
and I must choose to break their lucent shells.

SANDWICH

My artful sandwich lay on the plate,
arranged like a Paul Klee painting.
The purple and lavender of grape jelly
spread across sepia bread —
a perfect complement
to the slippery hard-boiled whites
and the soft ochre texture of yolks
with their green halos.

It seemed like
it would taste
as wonderful
as it looked.

My mother warned me,
if you make it, you have to eat it.

It took me all afternoon.
Art is sometimes hard to swallow.

Intent

After the heroine died, her priest said,
Let her be buried in sacred ground,
we recognize the baptism of desire.

I had always supposed that phrase
described passion and pleasure,
a vaguely liquid sexuality,

that we slept in a sacred place,
our bodies — you and I — a marriage of desire
washed in the blessings of love.

Are we anointed by our intentions,
sanctified or convicted by our desires?
If I long to kill you, have I?

Please let me know if you have died,
even a little, since your demise last crossed
my mind in a fleeting capital crime.

If immersion thought about, is done,
we can promise the heavens,
and though we are dry and desolate,

the sky will answer with miracles.
We can become vessels of god,
pour out our grief, bathe in its eternity,

or finger the edge of a Freudian slip —
maybe sense her name perfumed
between a silence in our bed.

Phenomenological theories negate intent,
leave it ground into the asphalt on the road
to hell — of course, without the evidence of hell.

We may be immersed in water,
but not baptized and certainly not
with desire or faith or slander.

I intended to love you,
to circle our bed with desire,
to wake beside you always,

but there was that odd tilt
to your head as you read
the morning paper.

Schrödinger's Cat

Petting the cat before dawn in winter,
      a flash, crackle, spark ignites my cold bedroom.
I think of this surprise on the way to work,
      and the steering wheel, the gas pedal, the brake —
how I am connected to this vehicle, think I control it,
and then I wonder how much sway I actually have.

A cat, startled by the shock
      of being stroked
on this brittle morning could shiver, whine,
race across a yard wondering why
      his master's hands, usually
      so gentle, were electrified today —
and this cat, set off by an ignorance of physics,
could run in front of my car,
      and I would hit the brakes, maybe swerve,
and then … the steering wheel that I trusted
      won't stop turning, or maybe the car has been coerced
by the natural spin of tires,
      hitting a stone but not the cat,
      who I missed, and who also seems
to have flown into a tree, and maybe that
is where I am going too — up in the tree
      with the static cat, without a plan, flying end
      over end like a hub cap out of control.

A physicist could predict the course of a body
      released from a wheel at forty miles per hour
      on a bridge with ten-foot concrete sections
      suspended thirty feet over traffic flowing

at five miles per hour — but with all these calculations,
I've lost track of the hubcap, and the cat,
        and am wondering if this steering wheel will ever stop
            turning, or if the cat is being propelled by dreams
        instead of terror, if there is a confusion of the two
            that doesn't affect the cat, but is whirling around me
while I am sitting still, but going a mile a minute.

If you could watch yourself from six feet back,
        you could see the off-kilter sway of your head,
            the way you beckon disaster without speaking —
        if you pet a cat at dawn and kindle the flash beneath his cheek.
It's all planned —
        you could watch those dendrites flare and fire along
            the paths in your brain and someone with a million,
million calculations could predict what will happen —
            but I can't.

If it's not thought out, and practiced,
        I become that shiny disk spinning
            in an endless dream of highway,
        the dark slapping me with headlights,
            cats in the swale, so close,
                spill of searchlights to the south,
        sheath of night wrapping me
            in a moon fuzz of winter green.

The next morning still arid, still gray.
Before I bare my feet to the cold floor,
        I pull a woolen sock out of another sock —
            it glows like a lantern and crackles
                over the sheets, over the sleeping cat.
I wake him up,
        stroke his chin — waiting,
            waiting for the spark.

There is No Atmosphere on Mars,

no lounge lizards,
no dimly lit pianos,
no film-noir shadows
slaking over scarlet dust,
no neon air to inhale smoke,
no stratosphere of clouds banking beyond the horizon
as the Martian axis twists and gravity crushes legend.
No Spanish moss bangling its southernmost oaks,
no magnolias to weave the lush thread
of photosynthesis into a tapestry of hungers.
No vapor from sizzling Martian rain,
lifting, red and passionate, into the sun's assault.

It is a place without illusion,
where a thready pattern of canals
tempts us to remember Venice,
but no lines slip from verbal to incredible,
no monologues bounce and sink
into fresh mimosas or gin and tonic.
No heroes slouch in the back booth.
No doomed blondes with finger waves
whisper secrets before they die.

Spy

I am a spy with secrets in my purse,
      lipstick that sees around corners,
         cigarettes that put the room to sleep.
Every doorway seeps adrenaline,
      every street, a question of national security.
When I am good,
      we all have dinner
         at a four-star restaurant.
When I am bad,
      someone dies.

I can change identity inside a cell phone,
wire bugs and bombs, sip martinis with tiny onions
      at chic night spots. I am the heroine, the liar, the thief,
the zip-lipped lover with red herrings
      and counterspies in my date book.
I am fabricator, searcher, puzzler, lock pick,
computer whiz-bang girl in go-go boots and a trench coat.

I hide my transmitters,
      encrypt what I say in punk jargon,
      and report everything I see to the home office:
         the klutzy ballerina, the gymnast who can't jump,
      the misplaced tuxedo, torn sheets,
         the dying mother
            whose secret Armenian lover betrays her
         in the last great starvation of minds.
I am the bookish one peering over these pages,
so no one will suspect my real mission.

In my other life, I am chameleon — and too wise
      to sleep at night without a small machine gun
         under my pillow. In another life,
            I always get my man.

RIDDLE

I was never where I said I was,

but followed a duality of choosing
without a thought
for who or why.
I scraped time
from a foggy windshield,
watched calmly
as a spider dropped
from the rearview mirror
into the lap of someone else

sitting where I said I was

at the Turnpike Drive-in Theatre
under a Necco Wafer moon
next to a sweating
papercup
gradually caving
in to the heat of Miami
and criss-crossing the parallels

of who I said I was
and where I really went.

Party Girl

If you are looking for the party girl,
        I think I lost her. She was riding
        the Ferris wheel of devotion, little cars of flirtation
        rocking back and forth above a life of crime,
     keenly observing breakage, and a tragic co-mingling
     with the DNA of others. She was listening to wiretaps
     of felonious delight, a coma of details descending into the room;
the sure knowledge that truth has crawled under the rug,
     is a spent bullet embedded in the wall to the left of her head,
        is shacked up with a former lover.

Be as generous as you can —
        if I give you my body or my bank account,
        which would lure you from the ledge of despair?
And if these gifts split my heart with their giving,
    how should I walk this indulgent tight rope — crouching like a cat,
        or with arms spread wide above the long bright fall?
I am in a reverie of small detail,
stacking gestures and innuendo
        to create a scenario I can live in.

Too bad she has forgotten all the names, closed her eyes
        when important things occurred,
        and now cannot separate the crimes from the miracles,
         cannot identify the criminal or the saint,
sits on the steps of a locked church,
wonders when god will open for business again.

In my mind, beyond the trees are city slums
        too dangerous for the uninitiated, too sullen for a party,
        rules of conduct succinct, but unwritten.

Angels wear blue, and flash a turban of lights into our flesh.

We are bereft at corner walk-wait signals,
adrift in dirty snow, trapped under the wheels of cars.

How powerful I am in memory,
        gentle suspicions, human sacrifice,
        racial slurs, rockets in the air.
Listen, human nature is rioting again.

IV.

DISBELIEF

Now And Then,

a plume of vermilion smoke blossoms,
etherizes in the sky.

What in us is silenced when we make
the violent beautiful, give it
the luster of polished stones?

What is buried has not left the earth
and may be resurrected,

may rise from the river
in a body we long thought dead.

The blood roils,
surrounds the bullets,
embraces them with flesh.

To die in such beauty —
the horror leaves our lips, quietly
lifting and swelling with the tide.

We watch, we watch,

and who can know
when to stop watching,

when to wait for the sky
to bloom again?

In Gaza

Despair climbs down from the window
and sleeps beside me while I count
the coins of silence stacking in the alley.

Windows and dishes are broken —
dusty shards of an ordered life
bleed in our front yard.

The boundaries of my neighborhood
creep back and forth like frightened roaches,
their dark feet skittering after curfew.

Concertina wire jewels the fence,
bangles in the searchlights
that spider our nights.

Old men wrap rags around their ideas,
give them crutches and send them
stumbling into the severed afternoon.

My tongue wraps around hate —
that ancient bone that feeds us,
chokes us, grows as we consume it.

The earth is cratered with doubt.
We steal bits of food from the ants —
a chorus of want sings in my fists.

Today her door was locked and crime-taped
after a man jumped from her crown —
a botched swan dive into the Hudson.

He imagined his body, a knife slicing into the water,
his heart bursting as the river took him in.
Instead, he snagged a guard rail and hit the rocks.
The elegant solution for ending his life
missed by several feet — isn't that always the way?
We have such visions for how things should be,
cycle conversation in our heads obsessively —
the one-sided dialogue unstoppable,
and the voice trapped inside
bouncing around like a crazed pinball.

What we will say, how we will look,
how glorious the comeback will be, could have been —
the reasoned explanations we silently tell ourselves
over and over and over until the telling
becomes the most unreasoned part of our life.

But the lady's golden door is closed
and the man has been scraped up and taken away.
The crowd is muttering —
thwarted from their vertical pilgrimage,
from the awe of remaining large
while those beneath us shrink.

We want to be at the top —
part of the flame, part of the burning,
but the door is locked. We wait.
No one has come to tell us
what is hidden in her robes.

Did he leave a note behind, have help?
Did tired climbers gasp at the last glimpse
of his worn soles pushing from the ledge?

We don't go home, we sleep at her feet
waiting for the door to open,
to climb inside her head.

like butter,
like paint spilled on polished granite,
like pollen riding a yellowish wind.

Grenade launchers blossom
on the shoulders of insurgents.
Magnetic fields attract Hummers and helicopters.

These tanks and drones had no where else to go today.
Tidal currents washed aircraft carriers into the Persian Gulf.
Soldiers wandered in like spreading rumors,

furtive rings on a pond overflowing,
filling ditches, surrounding hydrants
and lamp posts, concealing the road kill.

We witness the victory of chaos over prayer.

This year, evil is sand colored,
scrolling death tolls along the bottom
of our cool flat screens.

Our young targets, like lawns,
lie down beneath the mower.
A rain cloud may cross the desert.

Low-bellied snakes will drown.
We will float past perdition.
Winged creatures will redeem us.

Volition: possum asleep on the yellow line.

I watch an actor playing a witness lying to a detective,
       and try to decide whether she is lying,
           a weaving, wandering double helix
               of fact and fiction.
      Since the actor isn't talking now,
    but watching her detective circle the room,
      I watch her eyes watching the detective
        watching her.
He's thinking,
Everyone lies, but why is she lying tonight? About this?
        How can I get her to circle back to the truth?
And she is wondering how
    she ever got tangled into this web,
      how she loves the guy who could be guilty.
    She doesn't want what she says to send him to jail.
     She wants to give him an alibi,
       but she hasn't seen him since he abandoned
       a coffee cup in her kitchen two days ago.
She tells the detective her guy was in her bed —
    not because he was, but because she wishes he had been.

Of course these actors are on film,
    so the truth of their performance is preserved,
      can be rewound, watched again.
When does fiction become truth, cross over,
     suspend my disbelief?
     And, if I believe her,
    even though it may not be true,
     according to the script,
   I will be relieved when she goes home,
     and her guy is curled around his alibi
       and his kisses seem tender and authentic —
so intimate that I am kissed.
    If my disbelief were not suspended,
      I would wonder how they managed to act so privately

                    in a studio surrounded by a crew
        and painted backdrop of the New York skyline.
But now, my disbelief is real
        as I search for the twin silhouettes
        that guarded this city since 1973 and now
mark a gap in our perception
                    of what is permanent.

The detective never sees
                the truth of the kiss,
        or proves the alibi false.
The guy in the alibi bed is innocent,
            but would have been accused
        if his lover had not lied.
Of course, he lied to his lover about that night —
                never imagining that she wouldn't mind
                    if he stayed home to read a novel
                        instead of sleeping at her place.
If we paint the twin towers back into the backdrop,
            can we pretend for one night that they still exist,
        that we fell asleep before the film destroyed them,
                or that the hero was able to thwart the attacks
                    at the last minute by diverting the planes
                        to an airstrip across the Hudson River?

Or what if the witness tells another kind of lie
        and implicates her innocent lover,
        makes it possible that he is guilty
                because he lied to her about a book,
                and now she is lying too,
                placing him at the crime scene instead
                of reading Dostoevsky in his apartment.
        And here we imply that, ironically,
        he is reading *Crime and Punishment* —
so the fiction winds around another ring of truth

until we can't untangle it, the writer creating
a victim of an innocent fiction reader —
what could be more true, or false?

(Some might be reminded of a two-headed snake
coiled inside a murky Mason jar like a pickled egg
at a roadside attraction in Florida,
— a real snake in a real jar,
but we keep looking for the stitches
that join the two heads —
never quite suspending our disbelief, but also wondering
which head decided where to crawl
before the lid tightened
and the jar was placed on a shelf.)

The detective goes home after questioning the witness
and lies to his wife when she asks about his shift.
He doesn't want to let the shattered flesh
he examined at the crime scene invade his home,
doesn't want to say words that give the images power,
but his wife knows he is lying. She saw the blood
on the sidewalk during the evening news.
She saw her husband's shoes step into the red pool,
saw the tendons in his neck tighten
at the edge of the last frame
before the reporter cut
back to the studio.
But she lies about knowing this
and nods as he complains about the heat
and the witness he knows is lying about her lover,
and skirts around the blood
that has been on the sole of his shoe all day
and followed him home.

She knows that security is an illusion,
            has known since she first imagined a somber blue knock
                    in the middle of the night, her bathrobe gaping
                            at the news waiting under her front porch light.
She knows he is tracking blood into the house,
            but also — not blood, but the fear
                    of making mistakes
                            leaves the darkest stain.

The detective dislikes lying to his wife about the blood,
                    the fear, and sometimes tells his lies
            to other women, who listen and believe,
                    for even though his wife pretends to believe him,
                            he also knows — she doesn't.

And there is that gaping skyline.
Though he was far away that day in September,
            some part of him fell into the wreckage at Ground Zero.
He knows, when the audience watches him
            walk down a New York street,
                    they will check to see if the World Trade Center
                            is there,
whether this story is before
            or after
we changed our perception
            of what to disbelieve.

After "Wings of Desire"

I.
Angels, you have seen
the parting of the waters,
the stones assembling,
the first howl, the first word,
fires on the river bank,
the first zigzag of war,
the yellow stars
sewn on woolen coats.
Do you remember the stags
grazing where asphalt
now stretches over ancient grass,
the grass that always returns?

II.
Angels listen, and testify
that I have chosen the olives over the pear,
have wondered about the separation of flesh
and prayer, or pondered how inseparable
they must be, given the shape of my hands,
have closed an umbrella and let the rain
wash me as I stand on the gray sidewalk,
that I have let my soul drift on a trapeze
and slept with a wing brushing my cheek,
that I languish with the cats stretched
on the car like islands of silk,
that today I scratched charcoal
on rough paper, heard it cast its color
on the line of an old man's brow.

III.
An angel's hand on the window sill —
outside broad leaves interrupt
the falling rain, syncopate
with faster unfettered drops

drumming the ground.
A train whistle cellos
above the wet rhythm.
Angels thread around me
listening. They hear my stories,
but their numbers dwindle as they forsake
a life with wings for flesh,
for taste, for solitude.

IV.
Angel on my windowsill,
I have dreamed of you.
Come hang from my trapeze.
Sell your armor and drink coffee
with cream swirling
in the deep brown
cup of your eyes.
Taste rain, dust, blood.
Select a hat.
Juggle the pears,
or the olives.

Our collective unconscious has been spattered
with binary code. Thoughts fall black/white
into ether. We are not given to ambivalence.

We know exactly how right or wrong we are,
where we can go, and in a linear obtuseness,
we identify the void as part of our secret code.

Gazing into certainty, we do not question
what formed our minds —
fingers frantic to create life,

we are too busy birthing an artificial
intelligence to bring forth our own,
to play the unconscious for our best vibes.

A string of numbers
tangles our ideas of god,
identity, impropriety.

Black and white piano keys
up down, off or on,
adagio, allegro —

we strike the screen.
Identity thieves come after us,
slip away with our codes,

and some believe these numbers
have become our souls, our bodies,
our selves — that we are binary beings,

biped, bionic, bisexual, biodegradable,
bipolar, bioterrorist in the airplane,
evil, not evil.

V

ENTANGLEMENTS

Diary

When I was young, I dreamed an ancient fog
       cloaked the river between us,
that stones remembered our fingers,
though we were still unformed
       and had lived without tools in our hands.
I was grateful for their chiseled faces.

I have saved the dust.

I heard the ocean quietly tonguing the shoals,
       seaweed drifting like Samson's hair,
       braiding the sand where it slid ashore.
Gulls on tiny feet minced and pecked in the foam.

I dreamed I was a boat.

I found hills that leaped into the horizon,
       ribboned with roads around the sun.
Hooves of rebellion beat in each restless finger.
How I yearned to conquer the road, to follow it into my life.

I cut my foot. I built a house instead.

The road curled into itself.
I lost my way in a labyrinth of habit,
       fretting in dark tunnels of domesticity.
         How quiet I was.

Shall I pursue my desires or slowly peel them off,
       like clothes dropping near a bed —
         first a sleeve of sensuality,
           a cuff of anger,
             collar of pleasure?

Disrobe. Leave nothing behind.

Sonata

Your index finger plays tiny sonatas
in the hollow of my collarbone
as the drone of amplified speech echoes
from podium to bare ceiling,
circling our baked fish in schools of thought.

We shift in these stick straight chairs,
too often hypnotized in the revolutions
of the ceiling fan click, click, clicking.

Your touch at my neck renders
a most tender annoyance.
When can I leave?
       Leave you.
Forget your fingers evolving into hands.

The microphone shrieks, it too wants to run.
I shrug. I cannot slump forward and leave
room for your arm beneath me anymore.
Its protection leaves me misshapen.

I let go of your index finger, your thumb,
your circling shoulder. It is not enough,
      it is too much, too warm
          and now,
I wish to be cold and still.

You say, *How can you leave now?*
Later dancing. Stars. It's what we came for —

a measure of sky reflected in the water,
our silhouette shimmering at the end of the dock.

A Bell, My Breast, My Flesh

                    blessed with salt.

Sexton to the night-birds
and demons sleeping in uncertain shoals.

My fingers find my other hand
                    stroke like one dark feather.
Skin, the cloth of illusion,
                    aria inside my palm resonating,

                                        gathering power,
                    bright clutch, sweet fist —
                    my flesh shall sing.

Flesh
        that betrays
                    and shreds,
        cloak that tears away,
                    that rents and billows in a terrible sea.

Single turn of my thumb and forefinger,
                    sound that splits an atom of twilight.

The mystery that flesh is bound,
                    yet free.

Once

Once, I was almost beautiful.
Now, a folded envelope,
brisk walk to the mailbox,
a tendency to abbreviate my name.

I was, once, almost appropriate,
now, a rusted folding chair,
walking stick of sorrow,
a slowly wrought tenet of discontent.

Now, an inappropriate silk
chemise draped slyly over a chair,
no longer chasing sorrow, or
the slowest unraveling of day.

Yesterday, a silk web fell,
drifting over my ledge —
a chastened end to prayer,
unraveled truth in thin, sad strings.

Thursday falls like salt,
adrift on a plate of mirrors.
A praying hand will drop away
like trust in the lies of belief.

Tomorrow, a salted beauty,
a mirror of cracked reflection,
frozen gestures fading away,
beliefs in tangled frenzy.

Once, a beautiful remnant,
a reflection in folds of salt.
Now, a gesture of smoke,
a tangle of silk and moon.

Tomorrow, a remnant of sorrow
a fold in sallow paper,
then, a letter writ with smoke
across the moon's dark sea.

Now I am breath and sorrow,
paper and ash and heartbreak.
My home lies west of Lethe,
a sea of disbelief.

Tomorrow I will breathe
and break the broken chair.
Home is a sorrowed ghost —
belief, a sullen prayer.

and the days were half as long?
My body and yours,
your eyes and my lashes,
my thumb

and your hand
as you lift a cup of ginger tea,
warm and lingering
as it slides down my throat.

The sky like days
crawling into our bed.
Twilight, a blister
rising beneath the trees,

and our conversation
murmuring past midnight,
silence excised
as I hear your blood

rumbling in my veins.
Our memory intermingled —
your father, my father
like a chair with four legs.

What if you and I were a rapture
of singular bliss — a kiss
so intrinsic that we become
the antithesis of longing?

How would we find ourselves
with only two eyes?

You and I. We, us.
One, gone.

DESTINATION

Goldenrod nodding in the swale,
      roadside conversation flicks too fast for translation.
         Armadillo upended, legs thrust into a metal sky.
      Cotton bolls litter the ditch for miles,
        angel fluff that fidgets as I whir along.

The journey, a long sentence of rain and red lights
        hazing through the wipers.

Driving toward solitude,
        like it is a destination
            surrounded by mountains.

Confusing loop of highways,
      the map, a soothsayer
        with dangling bracelets of red and blue roads
                twisting at her wrist.

It is
    so
      quiet, I can hardly lift my pen to scratch away the silence,
        the Sequoias in my dreams are falling.

Footsteps echo on the gravel at dusk,
        syncopate with the bounce of the flashlight beam.
      Solitude has glowing eyes, slithers and shakes in the underbrush.

I let my mourning pour into Betty's Creek,
        slide down the mountain —
             my father, my father.
    At the bend of the road,
a crimson barn — spotted cows with young calves.
      New life beckons.

TRACE

I trail my fingerprints, my epithelials,
    my hair, my spit, footprints, and sweat behind me —
  unintentional traces, evidence of my disassembly,
     mysteries.

My hair weaves a random weft around my comb.
   Evidence tangles silently in the bathtub drain.
My life is not a crime scene,
  except for all those small indiscretions —
    words thrown like small daggers,
    yellow lights that turn red too soon,
    cat pushed roughly off the bed.

What traces do our thoughts leave?
  The universe expands —
    the membrane of consciousness
      bulging across the cosmos,
      filling with memory,
      with the debris of experience.
 Our sorrows beaded into the belt of Orion,
    the subconscious finally an equal —
    psychic pleasures balanced with carnal knowledge.

I left without a trace,
  drove away, taking my DNA, my chemical profile,
    my fingerprints and voice print,
    my toothbrush and hairbrush,
    dental records and X-rays,
  every photograph.

I shredded my ID cards, resumes and transcripts,
          income tax forms, credit cards and life insurance.
I am watching my identity wither and evaporate —
                    no one knows me.
I burned down the house,
              sold the car to a broker
                        from Venezuela.
I left the genius of felines, a whiff of charisma,
          the complexity of a thought,
              a breeze of discontent.

Fog

Not cat feet, but grand leonardo-mona-lisa light
seeps into our faces, as air washes
the cupola on our cheap motel.

What is behind, revealed more in haloes
and peacock flames, is a place
where moths confuse the darkness.

The fine rain lost in light, wandering
in the live oaks, pulls fingers through
harp-vines of air, lies down on hollow streets,

tells us how the world darkens
and remembers how we lost
our haloes to indefinite dragons.

We glow within the paste of air.
Inky oak and fuzzy ellipses
punctuate the streets,

feeding the mysterious fish of trees
haloed in the burgeoning,
swimming dark.

Tomorrow the definite light
will return and scrub
our mystery from the air.

Inside our cheap motel, dark air reclines
on rumpled love-soaked sheets. We disrobe
in the halo of streetlights and drink a trembling sky.

Before

i.
Before I dreamed this,
it might have been true.

Before you confessed,
I was bound to you
with silken neckties,
tender threads that unraveled
with each revelation.

Before you lied,
I lived in another world,
secured with promises,
with obligations,
with sweet honey spread
on my morning toast.

Before I closed my door,
I let you in, to roam my body,
to shape my hands,
to shudder and weep at my side.

Before you left,
the blinds were open,
sliced your sleeping form
with the rap of woodpeckers,
squawk of jays, the yip,
yip of the neighbor's dog.

ii.
Before the hawk
flew against my window,
startled, and perched there,
wondering at the illusive
barrier of the glass.

Before I imagined my car could fly,
could sail off that mountain highway
and follow the hawk,
before I realized it couldn't,
and granted the road its hold.

Before September, before the air wriggled
like tiny fledglings in the tangles of their nest,
before the rain, the steam rising in parking lots,
the sauna of souls escaping.

iii.
Before I lay down in many beds,
before I knew my skin was porous,
that my mouth would mimic
whoever whispered in my ear.

Before you went back to your wife,
before I knew you had a wife,
before the mouse surprised me
in your bath tub, before I trapped
his small squirming body with a washcloth
and released him through the window,
before that — I was not who I became.

Before I was a giraffe, throwing back
my head to call to my own,
before I was in Africa, wandering,
my spotted heart drumming in the acacia trees.

Before skin and blood,
before breathing, before the conception
of sound, of thought,
                    I may have loved you.

FULL MOON

Full moon, ex-husband
sleeping in the guest room.

A wild road winding
        through the suburbs —
                possum, fox, stray cats
                dart into snarled underbrush,

cold, spring breakfast of his regret.

Japanese magnolia a cappella,
symphony of pink petals playing across the lawn.

Winter is unfinished.
        With so many years of forgetfulness,
walls fall.
        We see behind the doors we shut,
                the illusive measure of our neglect.
                The will to embellish anger, gone.

Someday, Vermeer will paint the light
        falling through my window,
                brush closed a door
                        to this other world,
                stroke highlights from an unseen sun
                        across an unmade bed,
                        across the moon's face,

twenty years of separation.

Naming

If I name this grief,
define it
with guilt
and redemption,
call it drowning,
desolation,
call it
fire and stone,

then I am bound
to care for it,
like a stray cat I name,
that demands I feed him.
He comes and goes,
sometimes disappears
for days and then returns,
insisting that
I remember.

MY BODY CONFOUNDS

this body,
        my body
                confounds,
its tender contours
        without clues.

I dream of running —
        trapped in Ophelia's rags,
            forget the door is closed.

My fingers dance without a partner,
      stealing lovers out of books,
      finding lies to sleep with.
      The sun sets without invitation,
          no howling, no trumpets,
          even geese leave silently,
          their line slowly adjusting to their migration,
          their corridor crowding
              a sky once vast,
              now empty only for a moment,
      sweet, sly, sinking moment
      when stars huddle in constellations,
          and blankets congregate at my feet.

Dragon of swift things consumes us so quickly
      we do not know how to change,
      to be swallowed by fate,
      become the food of prayers
      sly sweet potions on our tongues

Remember the caged monkeys.
        Behind a forest of green bars —
                so intent on slices of dripping orange,
                they grabbed a bar and flew to the next,
                gymnasts, trapezios, flying Wallendas.
Remember the tall barn —
        inside, the giraffe with her newborn,
        all legs and splayed amazement.

I save feathers dropped in the yard for some soft gift —
whose hands should hold these plumes of owl and jay,
                        trail of lost wings?
        See, I am dreaming of flamingoes balanced on one leg,
                silent flames of feather.

I step over slanted sidewalks, ladders of transformation,
        hills of parking ramps and stolen asphalt,
        chutes of rain like wet daggers,
        apse of worry, cathedral of arrogance,
        clerestory windows shafting light,
        charming quill of doubt.

In praise of level ground,
        the solid greeting of earth beneath me —
                my true compass.

Small prayers
        one word long, fireflies,
unwritten poems.

Maxwell's Demon Bends the Arrow of Time

*Maxwell's Demon: James Clerk Maxwell describes a microscopic
demon that guards a gate between two halves of a room. It lets only
slow molecules into one half, only fast molecules into the other half.
One side of the room becomes cooler than before, the other hotter.
This reduces the entropy of the room, and reverses the arrow of time.*

In this world, our acts proceed
from ending, rewind to meet the past.

An extinguished candle glows —
breath brings forth the light.

Our poems are spoken, for they
disappear as we write the words.

Photographs return to the sun,
fading as the shutter clicks.

A handkerchief drifts up, into our hand,
as we recall it dropping.

Acts of symmetry become sacred ceremony —
a convergence of future and past.

A kiss begins apart — a caress of lips —
and then, we part again.

From silence, we sing, and then
we are silent again. No one can sing forever.

Our souls grow both innocent and wise,
and our bodies lithe — enraptured in flesh.

In this perfection,
we ascend.

Electric Hair

I have electric hair
and wild fingers that zap the night.
I hurl cosmic fury at the stars
and paint neon graffiti on moonrocks.
My hair is schizophrenic,
soft as angels' breath
whispered on your pillow
and jagged as pink lightning
drumming its erratic cadence
across the midnight sky.
My hair is invisible,
twirling batwings in the wind,
haunting linens and lips,
a crown I only see in mirrors.

Once I tied our hair
together
in a tiny single knot.

It was an elusive, elegant union.

Carol Lynne Knight is the co-director of Anhinga Press, where she edits books and designs covers and text. She has worked on more than 100 literary publications, including books by Naomi Shihab Nye, the late Robert Dana, Diane Wakoski, and Judith Kitchen.

Her poetry has appeared in *Louisiana Literature, Tar River Review, Poetry Motel, Earth's Daughters, The Ledge, Slipstream, Broome Review, Comstock Review, Northwest Florida Review, Epicenter, Redactions, Iconoclast, Epicenter, HazMat, So to Speak, J,* and in the anthologies *Off the Cuffs* (Soft Skull Press), *Touched by Eros* (Live Poets Society), *The Poets Guide to the Birds* (Anhinga Press), *Beloved on the Earth,* (Holy Cow! Press), and *North of Wakulla* (Anhinga Press). She is a winner of the Penumbra Poetry Prize and has been nominated for a Pushcart Prize. She is the co-editor of *Snakebird: Thirty Years of Anhinga Poets.*

Born in Michigan, she grew up in South Florida and graduated from the University of Miami and Florida State University with degrees in Art Education. She is a fellow of the Hambidge Centter for the Arts. She has exhibited her drawings, pottery, sculpture and digital images throughout the eastern United States. In other lives, she has worked as an art teacher, potter, videographer, copy writer, and graphic designer. She has one son, who lives in Denver. She lives in Tallahassee, Florida.